of t

by Carolyn Thomson and Gordon Graham

DEPARTMENT OF CONSERVATION AND LAND MANAGEMENT

The ancient Kimberley landscape is punctuated with astonishing gorges and waterfalls, lush rainforest patches and wide expanses. Wherever you go in the region, birds are visible and abundant. Around 300 species of bird can be found at various times in the Kimberley. These range from typical birds of northern Australia, like the lorikeet and jabiru, birds found across the whole continent, such as the emu, and visitors from the north, such as the channel-billed cuckoo. Bird life includes rare Gouldian finches and purple-crowned fairy-wrens, waders that have flown vast distances from places as far afield as Siberia and waterbirds that breed on lagoons and lakes that form in the wet season.

Birds, such as the brolga with its elegant dance routine, are an integral part of both the mythology and natural environment of Australia's top end. Others like the little corella descend en masse into trees, clothing the branches with white. Such flocks of little corellas are a fairly common sight in the Kimberley, especially around dams and bores and at Windjana Gorge. Budgerigars are particularly abundant in the dry season, when observers will be enchanted with flashes of brilliant colour, as the flocks manoeuvre speedily and quite raucously across the countryside.

In the Kimberley, there are a number of places where birds can be seen in extraordinary abundance. Near Broome, the Royal Australasian Ornithologists Union bird observatory at Fall Point is an ideal place to view the waders which harvest the mudflats and tidal areas. The Parry Lagoons Nature Reserve, between Kununurra and Wyndham, is an important area for waterbirds. During the wet season, flooding creeks and tidal overflows from the Ord River inundate the flat, low-lying plain and bring abundant food to the lagoons and billabongs; food which attracts an incredible number and variety of waterbirds. Here, herons, ibises, many species of waterfowl, magpie geese and stilts can often be counted in their thousands. However, at any time of year near a waterhole, on a mudflat or near stands of flowering trees, a few minutes patient waiting will bring undoubted rewards.

It is hoped that *Common Birds of the Kimberley* will enrich people's experiences of the amazing Kimberley environment, by enabling visitors not just to identify some of the more common birds but to learn about their habits and life history.

KEY TO SYMBOLS

Habitat and food keys are provided for each species, with the appropriate symbols highlighted.

HABITAT

woodland   low woodland   spinifex grasslands   seashores & mudflats

lakes & rivers   streamside vegetation   rocky hills

FOOD

small animals   invertebrates   plants   fruits   flowers   seeds

MAGPIE GOOSE

(Anseranas semipalmata)

Hundreds of these birds will often flock in the shallows of rivers, drawing attention to themselves with their loud honking. You can gain an idea of the age of a magpie goose by the knob on the top of its head. The older the bird, the bigger the knob. It is usually larger on males. A male may only have one partner but will often divide his attentions between two females.

DESCRIPTION: These large birds are between 710 and 920 millimetres long. Males are somewhat larger than females, but both sexes are otherwise similar in appearance. They have a black head and neck. Around the hooked bill and eye the skin is bare and grey in colour. Their upper back, breast and undersides are white and the tail and lower back is black. They have yellow legs, feet that are half-webbed and large rear toes.

STATUS AND DISTRIBUTION: This bird ranges across the top end of Australia and down the eastern coast, but it has almost disappeared from southern Australia because of shooting, poisoning, drought and habitat reduction. Though still common in northern Australia, its numbers are in decline.

PREFERRED HABITAT: In the Kimberley it mainly inhabits coastal and sub-coastal plains. During the wet, it breeds in swampy areas such as Parry Lagoons Nature Reserve and around Lake Argyle.

LIFE HISTORY: Magpie geese nest on a deep, thick cup built within clumps of rushes. If the male has two mates they will share a nest, laying six to nine eggs each. The newly born geese only stay in the nest for a day before they learn to feed on shoots and seeds, with help from their parents. As the water recedes, the geese move with it - if the water disappears before the young are fledged they will die. The young can fly at 11 weeks, when they form flocks,

Photo – Jiri Lochman

which feed on nearby plains. In the dry season they can sometimes be seen digging out the edible bulbs of the spike-rush.

CALL: They make a loud honk, which may be repeated a number of times. Other birds may join in.

PLUMED WHISTLING-DUCK

(Dendrocygna eytoni)

This attractive duck makes a whistling sound during flight, hence the name. It is one of few ducks that doesn't appear to be entirely at home on water. It eats grasses and other plants, sometimes travelling more than 30 kilometres from water to feed at night. It also nests on land. By day the birds congregate on the ground near wetlands, sometimes in large numbers.

DESCRIPTION: These large ducks reach a maximum length of 615 millimetres for males and 560 millimetres for females. They are light brown on the head and neck, though the feathers on the back of the head and neck are darker. On each side of the breast is a large chestnut patch with attractive black bars. The belly and undertail is a brownish-yellow colour, with long black markings along the edge of the feathers on the flanks. The back and tail is dark brown, while the legs and feet are pale pink. Its bill is pink, mottled with black, which distinguishes it from the wandering whistling-duck.

OTHER NAMES: Plumed tree duck, grass whistle-duck.

STATUS AND DISTRIBUTION: Plumed whistling-duck is found in a very broad band across northern Australia and around the eastern coast, apart from closely settled areas. It has, however, increased in number since European settlement.

PREFERRED HABITAT: In the Kimberley, this bird favours well-watered tropical grasslands and can often be seen around billabongs, such as Parry Lagoons Nature Reserve near Wyndham.

LIFE HISTORY: During the wet season plumed whistling-ducks travel reasonable distances inland seeking food, but stay nearer wetter areas along the coast during the dry. The males begin to compete for the females with the onset of the first storms. After

the birds pair off, eight to 14 eggs are laid in a sheltered, grass-lined scrape in the ground. Both parents help incubate the eggs and care for the young.

CALL: These birds make a high-pitched whistling or twittering, both in flight and at other times.

DARTER

(Anhinga melanogaster)

With only its head and neck rising from the water, the darter resembles a snake. This waterbird submerges its body and quietly stalks its prey, then suddenly strikes with its S-shaped head and neck. Small fish, insects and other small aquatic animals are the targets of these unwelcome attentions - they are speared with the sharp, pointed bill.

DESCRIPTION: These large, supple birds are between 850 and 900 millimetres long. The males are predominantly glossy black. A long white strip, however, extends from the bill below the eye and along part of the neck. The upper wings have grey streaks, which can be seen to great effect when their wings are stretched out to dry. The females are greyish-brown above and paler below, with dark edges along the white head stripe.

OTHER NAMES: Snakebird, diver.

STATUS AND DISTRIBUTION: The darter is found throughout most of the Australian mainland, apart from a few arid central parts.

PREFERRED HABITAT: These birds inhabit lakes, rivers, swamps and estuaries.

LIFE HISTORY: Darters are closely related to cormorants. The males select and defend a nest site and build a rough platform of twigs. They attract females by waving their wings alternately. Four or more eggs are laid, at intervals of two or three days and both parents sit on the eggs and brood the young in shifts, while the other collects food. Darters may breed in any month, but most nesting activity is in spring and summer.

CALL: On the nest, darters make a harsh, rolling "kah", oft-repeated and decreasing in volume. A clicking sound is made when not nesting.

AUSTRALIAN PELICAN

(Pelecanus conspicillatus)

Pelicans can often be seen on a hot day hitching a ride on spiralling thermal updrafts. The birds spread out from their colonies with slow and heavy wingbeats, searching out suitable updrafts. When one is found, the lead birds begin to circle, flapping their wings intermittently, rising steadily through the sky. Within minutes a "staircase" is formed, with 10, 20, perhaps 100 pelicans spiralling steadily upwards. When they reach a suitable height, perhaps thousands of feet, they peel off and glide towards their destination. In this way the birds avoid expending considerable energy needed to propel their bulk through the air by flapping.

DESCRIPTION: Pelicans are easily recognised by their bold, black and white markings, slaty blue legs, enormous bill with pink pouch and yellow eye-rings.

STATUS AND DISTRIBUTION: They are common throughout most of Australia and small numbers occur on islands to the north.

PREFERRED HABITAT: They inhabit fresh and saltwater lakes and estuaries, rivers, swamps and sea shores.

LIFE HISTORY: At times, groups of pelicans can be seen co-operatively fishing, driving their prey into shallow water and dipping their beaks into the water at the same time. The bird's pouch is used mainly as a "scoopnet" for catching small fish and shrimps, rarely for carrying them. The pouch is also used for catching rain. Its total capacity is seven litres! Northern colonies nest between February and September, but usually from June to August. Nests are little more than shallow scrapes on the ground, often lined with pieces of seaweed and discarded feathers. Two eggs are laid. Within a couple of weeks of hatching, the chicks gather in small mobs or "creches". They almost invariably nest on islands.

WHITE-NECKED HERON

(Ardea pacifica)

White-necked herons inhabit the temporary rivers and swamps of more inland areas. Only in times of drought do they appear in numbers near the coast. Their modus operandi is to wade around the shallows, poised to gobble up any small creature they manage to flush out. They prefer to perch or nest in open or bare trees. In flight, the white "windows" on the leading edge of the wing can often be seen.

DESCRIPTION: These large birds stand almost a metre high. They have a greyish-black body and white neck and head, though the front of the neck is decorated with fine black spots. The white breast and white bend of the wings can be clearly seen in flight. When flying, they fold up their long necks and tuck their heads in close to the body, trailing their long legs behind them. The tail is quite short. A patch of bare skin between the black bill and the eye may be blue or yellow.

OTHER NAMES: Pacific heron.

STATUS AND DISTRIBUTION: They range across most of Australia, absent only from central arid areas of WA. They sometimes wander as far afield as Tasmania, New Zealand and New Guinea.

PREFERRED HABITAT: These birds are quite nomadic and usually inhabit temporary inland rivers and swamps and wet grasslands.

LIFE HISTORY: White-necked herons dine on insects, crustaceans, tadpoles, frogs and fish. Their nests are a platform of sticks, placed in trees up to 30 metres above the ground. These usually overhang water. Both parents help to incubate up to six eggs. Breeding is related to the abundance of food but is usually in spring and summer.

CALL: These birds make a large croak and other guttural calls.

NANKEEN NIGHT HERON

(Nycticòrax caledonicus)

These large pale brown birds are sometimes disturbed by people approaching waterholes in the Kimberley, and flap, awkwardly at first, to a new rest. Nankeen night herons are the only Australian herons that are nocturnal. These predatory creatures stalk their prey in the shallows, often using their sharply pointed bills to stab fish, amphibians, crustaceans and large invertebrates. They sometimes steal the eggs and chicks of other birds.

DESCRIPTION: These birds are between 560 and 650 millimetres long. The crown and back of the head is greyish-black and two or three white plumes decorate the rear of the head. The neck is short, imparting a hunched appearance. Nankeen night herons have a cinnamon back and wings and a white breast and belly.

OTHER NAMES: Rufous night heron.

STATUS AND DISTRIBUTION: Nankeen night herons occur throughout Australia, but are absent from many of the more arid inland areas. They extend throughout the Kimberley and range as far as Indonesia and the Philippines to New Caledonia.

PREFERRED HABITAT: They inhabit permanent and semi-permanent fresh and brackish waters.

LIFE HISTORY: These nomadic birds breed in the basin of the Murray and Darling rivers in huge colonies that number tens of thousands and in smaller numbers in WA, including the Kimberley. After the males stake out nesting territories they perform ritualised dance and song displays to attract a mate. The bright yellow legs change to pinkish-red, the yellow eyes turn orange, and the facial skin becomes bright blue during courting. Pairs stay together only one season, raising two or three young on a messy tangle of twigs collected by the male.

Photo – Jiri Lochman

CALL: At the nest these birds produce throaty croaking, rasping, buzzing or clacking sounds, while the youngsters screech raucously. A croaking call can sometimes be heard as they fly out to feed in the evening.

STRAW-NECKED IBIS

(*Threskiornis spinicollis*)

Straw-necked ibises often fly in V-shaped formations. These birds can often be seen feeding methodically on lawns and other grassed areas in Kimberley towns. They are abundant and the most widely distributed of Australia's three species of ibis. They are named because of the straw-like feathers that hang from the neck.

DESCRIPTION: These reasonably large birds have a black head with a very long, curved and tapered beak. The neck is largely white, as is the breast, belly and tail. The back and the wings are a glossy bluish-black. During courtship they also develop red patches behind the eyes and on either side of the breast, but these quickly fade. The legs are red.

STATUS AND DISTRIBUTION: Straw-necked ibises are found through most of the Australian mainland. They are absent only from the central deserts.

PREFERRED HABITAT: They inhabit swamps, the margins of lakes, sea shores and even paddocks.

LIFE HISTORY: Straw-necked ibises breed in large colonies, building nests in suitable thickets or on islands within swamps. The nests are essentially a platform of sticks. The birds lay up to five eggs, which are incubated by both parents. They consume frogs, snakes, molluscs, water-dwelling invertebrates, caterpillars and grasshoppers. The courtship ritual is quite ceremonial and incorporates much bowing and preening. They also bow when changing shifts to incubate eggs and to the young before feeding commences.

CALL: They grunt in flight.

Photo – Geoff Taylor

JABIRU

(Ephippiorhynchus asiaticus)

Standing statue-like in the shallows of a northern swamp, the greenish-black sheen on this bird's neck is clearly visible and in stark contrast to the red of its long legs. The jabiru is Australia's only stork. It is large - growing to more than a metre long and 1.2 metres high. The name jabiru is a Portuguese word for stork. This bird is a little inelegant taking off, making two or three running jumps to help launch its heavy body from the ground. Once in the air it flies with consummate ease, alternately flapping slowly then gliding, perhaps soaring to several hundred metres.

DESCRIPTION: Jabirus have long, oversized black bills for scooping their food from the water. Their tail and part of their wings are black and their head and neck is greenish-black. Part of the back, wings, breast and a few tail feathers are white. The long, gangly legs trail behind the birds when in flight. Although both sexes are similar, they are easily distinguished by their eye colour; the males have dark eyes, while those of females are yellow.

OTHER NAMES: Black-necked stork.

STATUS AND DISTRIBUTION: In northern Australia this bird inhabits areas within reasonable distance from the coast. In WA, they are found north of Exmouth.

PREFERRED HABITAT: Jabirus live near lakes, swamps, freshwater pools and mangroves.

LIFE HISTORY: Usually seen individually or in pairs, jabirus breed from February to June. Their nests are massive structures of tangled sticks, reeds and grasses, placed in the top of a tree or large bush, usually near a swamp. Their favourite food is freshwater fish but reptiles, frogs, crabs and rodents are also eaten.

CALL: Normally silent.

19

OSPREY

(Pandion haliaetus)

The huge nests of the osprey can be used generation after generation and often reach up to two metres high. These massive domes of sticks and driftwood are usually lined with seaweed. Early seafarers thought they must have been built by a bird the size of an Andean condor. Although it is often incorrectly referred to as a sea eagle, the osprey is in fact a hawk.

DESCRIPTION: Mature adults are between 500 and 630 millimetres long and have a wing span of one and a half metres. The creamy white head is sometimes flecked with brown markings and a dark brown stripe runs on either side of the alert bright yellow eye to the neck. The underparts and legs are also creamy white, while the upper parts and upper wings are mottled light brown, dark brown and black. The bill is black and hooked.

OTHER NAMES: Fish hawk.

STATUS AND DISTRIBUTION: Ospreys are found around most of the Australian coast. In northern Australia, ospreys are quite common and they are moderately common in the south-west, but the species has declined in South Australia and no longer breeds in Tasmania, Victoria and New South Wales. This decline may be due to pollutants causing breeding failures and deaths, and reduced habitat because of removal of large nest trees.

PREFERRED HABITAT: The birds frequent offshore islands and coastal areas, and in the Kimberley also move inland up rivers and on lakes. Their nests can be seen in drowned trees at Kununurra and Lake Argyle, and along the Fitzroy River.

LIFE HISTORY: Fish are the staple diet. In the north ospreys breed between July and September, laying between two and four eggs. Aerial displays during courtship are quite spectacular. The

male hunts while the female incubates, broods and feeds the voracious chicks. The youngsters leave the nest about eight weeks after hatching.

CALL: Ospreys typically produce a short quavering whistle.

BLACK KITE
(*Milvus migrans*)

Black kites are the seagulls of the Kimberley. These scavenging birds are often seen around towns, especially near rubbish tips. They usually forage in flocks, or perch together in trees, seeking respite from the heat. Twenty to 30 of these birds will often follow fires spreading through savannah grassland, circling and dropping through the smoke in search of an easy meal.

DESCRIPTION: These birds grow up to 550 millimetres long. They are predominantly dark brown, with a lighter brown head and neck, wing patches and underparts. The tail has a shallow fork, and is constantly moving and twisting in flight.

OTHER NAMES: Fork-tailed kite, Kimberley seagull.

STATUS AND DISTRIBUTION: These birds are common through most of the Australian mainland, being absent only from south-western WA and a section of the east coast. They are also found in Europe, north Africa, southern Asia and New Guinea.

PREFERRED HABITAT: Black kites inhabit a range of habitats, including woodland and savannah areas, and can almost always be seen circling over Kimberley towns.

LIFE HISTORY: Although the bulk of their diet is obtained from scavenging carrion, black kites will sometimes swoop on live rodents, reptiles and insects, which may be swallowed in flight. They build a platform of sticks up to 30 metres above the ground on which to lay two or three eggs which are incubated by the female. During nesting the male obtains most of the food but does not directly feed the young. In the Kimberley, they usually nest between March and May, but also nest from August to September.

CALL: This bird makes a quavering "kwee-err" or series of staccato whistles.

WHITE-BELLIED SEA-EAGLE

(Haliaeetus leucogaster)

White-bellied sea-eagles can be seen on high vantage points near water or swooping on to fish or other prey, their powerful wings uplifted. They land on the ground to tear their prey apart with large talons. Tortoises, waterbirds, rabbits and carrion supplement the diet of fish. In the Kimberley these graceful creatures can be seen as far inland as Geikie Gorge, on the Fitzroy River, and Lake Argyle.

DESCRIPTION: Female white-bellied sea-eagles reach up to 840 millimetres long, whereas males have a maximum length of 760 millimetres. The head, neck, breast and underparts are snowy white, but sometimes have extremely thin, inconspicuous streaks of grey. The back, wings and tail are almost black. The tail, however, has a broad white tip.

OTHER NAMES: White-breasted sea-eagle.

STATUS AND DISTRIBUTION: It ranges around the entire Australian coastline and sometimes inland along rivers.

PREFERRED HABITAT: This bird favours sea shores and islands, following large rivers and lakes inland. In fact it inhabits most places with extensive water. In the Kimberley it can sometimes be seen near colonies of fruit bats, on which it preys.

LIFE HISTORY: Sea-eagles build enormous nests, up to four metres high, often perched on a cliff. Breeding is between May and October. Two eggs are laid, several days apart, but the first-born monopolises all the food and the second usually dies. The female spends the most time sitting on the eggs and brooding, only relieved for short periods by her mate. She feeds the nestlings with food captured by the father.

CALL: The call is a raucous "cank-cank-cank".

BROLGA

(Grus rubicundus)

No bird is more symbolic of northern Australia than the graceful brolga, one of only two species of crane in Australia. These tall birds are renowned for their elaborate courtship dances, which, however, are not confined to the breeding season. In the evening, pairs of these stately grey birds typically swoop over the top of tall paperbarks landing, with loud honking calls, near a waterhole. They face each other, spread their wings and dance.

DESCRIPTION: Brolgas generally reach more than a metre tall, with males slightly larger than females. They are whitish-grey over most of their bodies, though the primary wing feathers are dark. The head is bright red to orange, with a pale grey patch behind the ears and a pale grey forehead. The birds have a long, pointed orange beak and are supported by long, thin black legs.

OTHER NAMES: Australian crane, native companion.

STATUS AND DISTRIBUTION: Brolgas are found throughout most of northern Australia and across most of the eastern States (excluding Tasmania).

PREFERRED HABITAT: Swamps of coastal northern Australia.

LIFE HISTORY: When not breeding, family groups may converge into large flocks of several hundred birds that may move over large areas in search of food. The tubers of sedges are the most sought-after food item. Brolgas are graceful in flight and, like pelicans, make use of thermal updrafts to soar high into the air. They breed in shallow swamps in the wet, separating into pairs. Brolgas usually produce two young, nesting on a dry, grassy platform. The young are cared for by the parents for a year or more.

CALL: Brolgas call to each other with a trumpeting sound.

Photo — Jiri Lochman

AUSTRALIAN BUSTARD

(Ardeotis australis)

Also known as the bush turkey, the Australian bustard was a prized meal for early settlers. Grazing, predation by introduced foxes and hunting by people have all contributed to its decline. The Kimberley is now one of few areas in Australia where you can still see these majestic birds. A bird startled by an approaching vehicle will often launch itself into the air. Laborious, slow wing beats give the appearance of a great unwillingness to fly.

DESCRIPTION: These birds may grow up to 1.2 metres, with a 2.3 metre wingspan. The females are smaller. The back, wings and tail are brown, part of the wing is black and white. The breast, belly, face and neck is cream and they have a brownish black cap.

OTHER NAMES: Bush turkey, kori bustard, wild turkey.

STATUS AND DISTRIBUTION: Bustards were once common throughout Australia's mainland. They have now disappeared from closely settled areas, such as the south-west of WA, and are uncommon elsewhere. However, they are still sighted frequently in the Kimberley and other drier parts of north-western Australia.

PREFERRED HABITAT: Open country, such as grasslands or shrublands, is preferred.

LIFE HISTORY: The males try to impress females during courtship by inflating their neck feathers into an apron, raising and spreading their tail and strutting about noisily. One or two eggs are usually laid on bare ground among grass. The female incubates the eggs and raises the young. Australian bustards feed on grasses, seeds, fruits, small mammals and insects such as grasshoppers. They are nomadic and move to areas of good rains.

CALL: They may make a low booming or a loud roar when breeding but are otherwise silent.

WHIMBREL

(Numenius phaeopus)

Every year, the whimbrel makes a remarkable journey. It nests in the tundras of the Arctic circle in June. After breeding, it makes its way over many thousands of kilometres, via the rice fields, lakes and beaches of eastern Asia, arriving in Australia's northern coast in late August or early September. It is one of several waders from Siberia that make the trans-continental journey.

DESCRIPTION: Whimbrels are reasonably large, 400 to 430 millimetres long. They are a mottled mid-brown and white, with largely white underparts. They have a long downward curving bill. They resemble the eastern curlew but are smaller and have two dusky stripes on the crown.

STATUS AND DISTRIBUTION: These migrants are found in coastal areas of most of Australia, including the eastern coast of Tasmania. However, they are reasonably abundant in the north and quite rare in the south. At low tide, they can be seen on the mudflats near Broome or from the jetty at Derby or Wyndham.

PREFERRED HABITAT: Whimbrels favour estuaries and mangrove mudflats.

LIFE HISTORY: Small flocks of up to 50 whimbrels can be seen combing through mud in coastal shallows to extract tasty worms, molluscs, crustaceans and insects. They make the return journey to the Arctic in late April to May but some individuals, especially immature birds, will remain in Australia.

CALL: When alarmed, whimbrels make a high "ti-ti-ti-ti-ti".

COMB-CRESTED JACANA

(Irediparra gallinacea)

Comb-crested jacanas are also called "Christbirds", lilytrotters or lotus-birds. Their exceptionally long toes help them balance on the leaves of water lilies, so that they appear to walk or run on water, flicking their tails as they go. Their other distinctive feature is the fleshy red comb that adorns the head. When they become excited this may turn yellow, as the blood drains out of it.

DESCRIPTION: These birds have black feathers on the crown, back of the neck, breast and tail. The wings and back are brown, and the neck and underparts are white. There is a black line from the bill to the eye and faint yellowish patches behind the eye and on the lower neck. Females are about 50 per cent larger than males.

STATUS AND DISTRIBUTION: They are common throughout coastal and near-coastal parts of northern and eastern Australia, from the Kimberley to northern New South Wales.

PREFERRED HABITAT: Comb-crested jacanas show a preference for deeper, permanent freshwater swamps and billabongs.

LIFE HISTORY: Jacanas eat mainly aquatic plants and insects, foraging alone or in pairs. They sometimes stop to sunbathe, lying on their sides on top of water-borne vegetation. The birds aggressively defend their territory from other pairs during the breeding season, which lasts from January to May. Jacanas nest on water at least a metre deep, building a platform of matted plants to support the eggs. Both males and females care for the young birds. If the water level rises or falls significantly, the parents will sometimes move their eggs and young by carrying them under their wings. If disturbed or threatened by a predator, both the adults and young can dive underwater and remain motionless for up to half an hour with only their bill and nostrils exposed.

Photo – Raoul Slater

CALL: They make a trumpet-like call when alarmed and a squeaking "pee-pee-pee" call to communicate.

BLACK-WINGED STILT
(*Himantopus himantopus*)

Black-winged stilts wade through muddy shallows in search of tasty morsels, their slender, red, stilt-like legs elevating them above the water line. Molluscs, aquatic invertebrates and small crustaceans are the most sought after items. They sometimes maximise their catch by foraging, spaced out in family parties of two or three. Several hundred such birds may gather loosely in the one area.

DESCRIPTION: Black-winged stilts are attractive in their simplicity. These birds are mostly white, with a black nape, back and wings. The rear of the neck, the eyes and the long narrow bill are also black.

OTHER NAMES: Pied stilt, longshanks, white-headed stilt.

STATUS AND DISTRIBUTION: Black-winged stilts are found throughout most of Australia, absent only from a portion of the arid central interior, where there are few permanent wetlands.

PREFERRED HABITAT: They inhabit the edges of muddy freshwater wetlands.

LIFE HISTORY: Black-winged stilts will nest in swampy vegetation, on islands, or on a muddy depression at the water's edge. Twigs and other vegetation are often used to build up the nest site into a platform. Four eggs are usually laid and incubated by both parents. The young leave the nest within hours of hatching, but are brooded each night.

CALL: This bird makes a yelping noise that sounds like a puppy. When in flight it makes a high-pitched piping call.

BLACK-FRONTED DOTTEREL

(*Elseyornis melanops*)

Black-fronted dotterels are often seen scampering along the shoreline. When approached too closely, they take a short flight in an arc over the water, landing once again on the shore. The broad V on their chest is distinctive. These little birds have short legs and short bills and tend to take aquatic insects, crustaceans and sometimes seeds from the wet ground along edges of bodies of water, rather than wading through shallows. They are quite nomadic and are often found wherever there is temporary or permanent water, even well inland.

DESCRIPTION: These birds are only 160 to 180 millimetres long. There is a bright red eye-ring and a red bill that has a black tip. Both male and female birds have a black patch above the bill and a thick black eye band that extends to the edge of a broad, black V-shaped collar on the breast. The rest of the breast and underparts are white. The top of the head, the back and the wings are a streaky brown. However, the shoulders are chestnut, the rump is rufous and the flight feathers are black. The tail is black with white edges.

OTHER NAMES: Black-fronted plover.

STATUS AND DISTRIBUTION: They are reasonably common across most of the Australian mainland.

PREFERRED HABITAT: They inhabit the shores of freshwater swamps, lakes, streams and dams.

LIFE HISTORY: Black-fronted dotterels usually feed alone or in pairs. In the north, breeding takes place between May and September. They lay two or three eggs in a shallow depression lined with stones, shells and twigs. These may be on bare, caked mud, on a bank or a dry stony riverbed. Both sexes share parental duties. They may fake injury to distract potential aggressors.

CALL: These birds make a soft chizzing noise when courting and if alarmed. They make a "tip" to keep in contact when flying.

SPINIFEX PIGEON

(*Geophaps plumifera*)

These richly-coloured birds are easily recognised by their tall orange crest. They are desert specialists which live in arid spinifex grasslands, mainly surviving on the seeds of the short-lived herbs, grasses and legumes that sprout there after rains. Spinifex seed is also an important food when it is available. The birds do, however, need water to survive. These exquisitely marked birds often run off the track as vehicles approach. Their movements are slightly comical: the bobbing head appears to be synchronised with the rapidly moving legs like a wind-up toy.

DESCRIPTION: Spinifex pigeons have a bluish white forehead and a rust-red crown topped with a long, pointed crest. The rust brown back has darker scalloping and the rust brown wings have black and light grey barring. The breast of the Kimberley birds has a conspicuous white band and a white lower breast and belly (a red-bellied form occurs in the Pilbara).

STATUS AND DISTRIBUTION: Spinifex pigeons are common and live in most of the Kimberley region (apart from the far north), a large part of the Pilbara and across vast tracts of Australia's inland, taking in most of the Northern Territory.

PREFERRED HABITAT: They favour stony spinifex hills and grasslands, where there is access to water.

LIFE HISTORY: Spinifex pigeons usually forage in small groups of up to 15 birds. They are not strong fliers and usually only make short flights of up to 30 metres. They are able to reproduce in every month of the year but most breeding is from September to November. As with most desert animals, however, their breeding is closely tied to rainfall, when they quickly breed to repopulate an area. They line a scrape in the ground beside a spinifex hummock

with some grass. Two eggs are laid and incubated by both sexes.
The young fledge in only eight days.

CALL: These vary from repeated "ooms", to coos and clucks.

WHITE-QUILLED ROCK-PIGEON
(Petrophassa albipennis)

The white-quilled rock-pigeon is a typical bird of the Kimberley, being almost confined to the sandstone hills and cliffs of the region. The tumbled sandstone boulders of these areas are its favoured foraging sites and also offer suitable cover. When disturbed the birds will often remain perfectly still, hoping to blend in with the similar-coloured rocks. If they take flight, white patches can be clearly seen on the outstretched wings. When startled, they will often leave their perch with a loud clapping of wings.

DESCRIPTION: The birds are chestnut brown, with the lighter edges of the feathers giving a scalloping effect over most of the body. The rump and undertail is darker. A large white patch may be present on the wings. The throat is spotted with white and there is a white line above and beneath the eye.

STATUS AND DISTRIBUTION: This bird is common in the Kimberley and found in a small area of the Northern Territory.

PREFERRED HABITAT: They spend their time in broken sandstone hills and cliffs and are common in the King Leopold Ranges, Bell Creek Falls, Manning Creek, Mitchell Falls, Mirima National Park and Purnululu National Park. They will nest on the ground next to rocks and even on top of exposed rocks.

LIFE HISTORY: White-quilled rock-pigeons are seed-eaters. A sexually excited male bird will spread his wings, raise the feathers on his back and bow several times towards the object of his attentions, often while chasing her. These pigeons nest during the dry season, between April and October, laying two eggs in ledges and rocky crevices lined with spinifex stalks and twigs. Mother and father both assist in incubation and other nesting duties.

CALL: These birds produce a variety of cooing sounds.

41

PEACEFUL DOVE

(Geopelia placida)

The peaceful dove is a ubiquitous bird of the Kimberley. It is the source of the gentle cooing sound people usually hear when they set up camp. The courtship displays of the males involve bowing, tail fanning and flying steeply upwards and clapping their wings.

DESCRIPTION: These birds are between 200 and 220 millimetres long. Their upper parts are greyish-brown with black bars, particularly around the neck. The throat and upper breast are bluish-grey and the rest of the breast and the belly are pinkish-white.

OTHER NAMES: Zebra dove, turtle-dove.

STATUS AND DISTRIBUTION: Peaceful doves are common in most of the Kimberley, parts of the Pilbara and most of eastern Australia.

PREFERRED HABITAT: These birds favour well grassed woodlands with nearby water. They can also be seen in towns, feeding in parks and gardens.

LIFE HISTORY: Peaceful doves consume seeds from a wide variety of grasses and other plants, which are gathered from the ground. They usually forage in more open areas where it is easier to collect this food, such as along roadsides and in burnt areas. In the wet season they tend to move inland to more sparsely vegetated areas. While they usually feed in pairs or small groups they may gather together at areas with plentiful food and water. Breeding is not confined to any time of year, but peaks in March and April. Two eggs are laid on a platform of sticks placed in vegetation.

CALL: Peaceful doves make a variety of cooing sounds and have a very distinctive "doodle-doo" call.

LITTLE CORELLA

(Cacatua sanguinea)

These raucous birds form huge flocks that roam the countryside in search of food and water. They descend en masse into trees, clothing the branches with white. Such flocks of little corellas are a fairly common sight in the Kimberley, especially around dams and bores. The gradually increasing volume of noise from large numbers of these birds usually ensures people camping near waterholes have an early start to the day.

DESCRIPTION: These medium-sized birds are 350 to 420 millimetres long. They are white, with yellow below the wings and tail. The skin around the eyes is bare, and pale blue in colour, and the feathers between the beak and eye are reddish.

OTHER NAMES: Short-billed corella, bare-eyed corella, blood-stained corella.

STATUS AND DISTRIBUTION: Little corellas are common throughout the Kimberley, Northern Territory and parts of central Australia. They also range from Port Hedland south to the Irwin River. They can be seen and heard in large numbers at Windjana Gorge and similar areas in the Kimberley.

PREFERRED HABITAT: They favour trees along watercourses for roosting and nesting, and open grassy areas with low vegetation for feeding.

LIFE HISTORY: The little corella has a habit of chewing the inside of its nesting hollows, which are frequently within boabs or river red gums. The birds deposit two or three eggs on the chewed wood dust, about 100 days after the end of the wet season. They feed largely on seeds collected from the ground.

CALL: Little corellas are especially noted for making a raucous screech and a three syllable call while flying.

RAINBOW LORIKEET

(*Trichoglossus haematodus*)

Screeching flocks of rainbow lorikeets often fly overhead in the Kimberley, as they commute between roosting and feeding areas. They will sometimes travel long distances in groups of between two and 50. At their destination, trees in flower will suddenly become transformed with all the colours of the rainbow, as the birds move busily through the outer foliage extracting nectar from the blossoms. They are highly nomadic, following rivers and creeks for the blossom of cadjeput (*Melaleuca leucadendra*) and silky grevillea (*Grevillea pteridifolia*). They also like woollybutt (*Eucalyptus miniata*) and scarlet gum (*E. phoenicea*), both of which have showy orange blossoms rich in nectar.

DESCRIPTION: Rainbow lorikeets have a striking plumage of bluish-purple, reddish-orange and dark green. They are medium-sized birds, between 300 and 320 millimetres long.

STATUS AND DISTRIBUTION: The species is Australia's most widespread lorikeet. Its natural habitat ranges across the top end of Australia, from the Kimberley to Cape York, right down the east coast, across to South Australia and in north-eastern Tasmania.

PREFERRED HABITAT: Forests and denser woodlands.

LIFE HISTORY: Rainbow lorikeets have brush-tipped tongues for blossom feeding, which demands a lot of seasonal and daily mobility. Nectar and pollen are the staple diet, while ripened fruit, insects, larvae, part-ripened maize and cultivated flowers are eagerly sought. They roost and feed in flocks. They breed between August and January, usually laying two eggs in a hollow limb or hole within a tree close to water.

CALL: They screech continuously when flying and chatter shrilly during feeding.

RED-WINGED PARROT

(*Aprosmictus erythropterus*)

A flash of bright red, on the wing of this large parrot, is the first thing spotted as it forages in the foliage of a tall flowering eucalypt. Red-winged parrots are beautifully coloured. The males are bright green, with striking red wing patches, a black upper back and bright blue lower back. They have a long, full lime green tail, tipped with paler green.

DESCRIPTION: These medium-sized birds are about 320 millimetres long. The females and immature birds are paler, but still colourful. They are dull green with yellowish underparts, red patches on the wings and a pale blue lower back and rump.

OTHER NAMES: Crimson-winged parrot.

STATUS AND DISTRIBUTION: Red-winged parrots are common in northern Australia, Queensland and central New South Wales. They are also found in southern New Guinea. Travellers heading north to the Kimberley can expect to see them from about Samphire Flats.

PREFERRED HABITAT: These birds favour eucalypt-lined streams and lakes.

LIFE HISTORY: Red-winged parrots usually forage for seeds, fruits and flowers, in pairs or small groups. In flight, they have an erratic, strong wing beat. Five or six eggs are laid on a layer of wood dust inside tree hollows. The female alone incubates the eggs, and during this time is fed by her partner. Both parents feed the chicks.

CALL: They may screech harshly or make a "crillik-crillik" call in contact.

Photo – Simon Nevill

BUDGERIGAR

(*Melopsittacus undulatus*)

Despite this bird's small size, flocks of budgerigars in the wild are a spectacular sight. They are particularly abundant in the wet season, when observers will be enchanted with flashes of brilliant colour, as the flocks manoeuvre speedily and quite raucously across the countryside. Flocks of budgerigars are expert at taking off and flying in a perfectly coordinated manner, despite frequent mid-air twists and turns. They make flying visits to waterholes in the middle of the day, descending en masse and immersing their heads in water, before moving away quickly. "Budgies" are popular pets throughout the world.

DESCRIPTION: The breast, belly, upper tail and lower back are bright green. The tail feathers are bright blue and green with a broad yellow band. The bird's head, neck, upper back and wings are covered with yellow and black bars.

STATUS AND DISTRIBUTION: Budgerigars are common and widespread throughout Australia's arid interior.

PREFERRED HABITAT: They like sparsely timbered grasslands, mallee, mulga, spinifex grasslands and trees along watercourses.

LIFE HISTORY: Flocks usually number less than 100, but larger groups of many thousands are not uncommon. These nomadic birds move around the interior in search of an abundance of seeding grasses. Their breeding is also influenced more by the availability of food than it is by seasons. In good times they breed prolifically, producing several successive broods. They nest in hollows or holes, often communally, and produce up to eight eggs. During courtship and while nesting, the male feeds the female by regurgitation.

CALL: Flocks make a warbled "chrp" when flying and feeding. Before taking off and when alarmed they produce a "zit" sound.

GREY-CROWNED BABBLER

(*Pomatostomus temporalis*)

Grey-crowned babblers live in constantly chattering groups, that can be seen hopping through a bush then flying quickly to the next. Members of the group rarely stray far from one another. Family groups of around 12 are dominated by one breeding pair. The other members help with nesting and caring for the young. They all bring food to the senior female when she is nesting. The group has a defined territory of about 12 hectares, which it will vigorously defend. They probe debris on the ground and rough-barked trees for a variety of insects, spiders and small lizards.

DESCRIPTION: Grey-crowned babblers are approximately 250 millimetres long. They are largely greenish-brown, with a grey crown and white throat. WA birds usually have a reddish-brown breast, belly and flanks. The tail is black, tipped with white.

OTHER NAMES: Cackler, happy jack, dog bird, parson bird, grey-crowned chatterer.

STATUS AND DISTRIBUTION: These birds are widespread. In WA they are found from Yalgoo northward. They range across most of the northern half of Australia and down the eastern coast and are also found in southern New Guinea.

PREFERRED HABITAT: Grey-crowned babblers show a liking for open woodlands and streamside vegetation.

LIFE HISTORY: Grey-crowned babblers are quite long-lived birds. They are full of character. Squabbles often break out between neighbouring groups and chasing and other aggressive behaviour will continue for several hours. Quite large, elaborate domed nests, up to 500 millimetres wide, are constructed for roosting and to lay

eggs in. Occasionally a territory will have more than one breeding pair and the females will then share the one nest. Each bird will lay two to three eggs.

CALL: As the name babbler indicates, these are noisy birds. They will make a repeated "chuck" and "wee-oo". When alarmed, they produce a loud "shak" or "woo-oo". The song is a braying duet. The nestlings squeal.

GREAT BOWERBIRD
(Chlamydera nuchalis)

Male great bowerbirds collect a variety of white objects - such as snail shells, stones, bones and leaves - to adorn their bowers. The bowers are avenues of twigs and grass, often open at the top and usually hidden beneath low vegetation. The bower may be refurbished or a new one built near the same location each year. A male bird will attempt to attract a female by spreading the small patch of feathers on the back of his neck to reveal a lilac display. They mate within the bower, before she leaves to nest and raise their young on her own. He may mate with several females.

DESCRIPTION: These birds are 330 to 370 millimetres long. They have a quite drab mid-grey colouring, with darker brown scalloping on the wings and back. Males have a broad lilac band on the nape, but this is smaller and sometimes absent in females.

STATUS AND DISTRIBUTION: Great bowerbirds are found throughout tropical parts of northern Australia, across the Kimberley, the Northern Territory and Queensland.

PREFERRED HABITAT: They inhabit tropical woodlands, open forests and thickets.

LIFE HISTORY: These fruit-eaters may be seen in the crown of trees laden with fruit or near waterholes. They also take insects. The males tend their bowers for most of the year, but the breeding season is from August to February, usually from October to January. The females raise one or two young as single mums. The nests are between one and 10 metres above the ground, in trees well removed from the bowers of the males.

CALL: They may make a harsh wheezing rasp. Males will make a variety of sounds during the breeding season such as hisses, churrs and mimicry.

DOUBLE-BARRED FINCH

(*Taeniopygia bichenovii*)

These energetic and sociable little birds often form flocks of 40 or so. They feed, drink, preen and sleep huddled together in groups of up to six, crammed into a purpose-built nest. They mate for life and several pairs will often nest in the same bush.

DESCRIPTION: These small birds are 100 to 110 millimetres long. A striking black ring circles the white face and runs across the lower throat. Another black bar runs across the lower chest. The lower breast and belly are cream. The upper back and head are a greyish mid-brown and their brownish-black wings are covered with fine white spots. The tail is black and the bill is bluish-grey.

OTHER NAMES: Owl-faced finch, black-ringed finch, Bicheno finch, black-rumped finch, banded finch.

STATUS AND DISTRIBUTION: Double-barred finches are common in pockets of suitable habitat in a wide band across the top end of Australia and down the eastern coast.

PREFERRED HABITAT: They normally inhabit thickets within grassed woodland or open forest, where there is good access to water.

LIFE HISTORY: These ground feeders feast on seed and grain but also pluck insects from the foliage. Double-barred finches lay four or five eggs in a spherical nest with a side tunnel for entry and exit. This is built from grass and placed in small shrubs and trees, or in stumps and hollows. In WA breeding is usually from January to March. Both sexes incubate and care for the young.

CALL: Their song is a sequence of quite nasal notes. Other nasal calls are made and at the nest they produce a high-pitched squeaking.

LONG-TAILED FINCH

(*Poephila acuticauda*)

The typically stumpy tail of many finches is replaced in this species by one that is long and tapering. The largely grey and white markings of the long-tailed finch are set off by a contrasting bright yellow bill and quite reddish legs.

DESCRIPTION: These small birds are 140 to 150 millimetres long. They have a black throat patch, and a black band between the eye and the bill. Most of the upper parts are pale grey becoming darker and more brownish on the wings. Apart from a triangular black patch on the rump, the breast and underparts are otherwise white, and there is a long black tail.

STATUS AND DISTRIBUTION: This little bird is common through the Kimberley, the northern part of the Northern Territory and far north-western Queensland.

PREFERRED HABITAT: It prefers savannah grasslands of tropical areas, where it frequents watercourses lined with eucalypts.

LIFE HISTORY: These birds occasionally supplement their diet of ripe and half ripe seeds with flying insects, particularly during the breeding season. Male and female long-tailed finches are inseparable. Pairs spend a considerable amount of time preening each other and rarely stray more than a metre apart. A number of pairs usually combine to form small flocks. They breed between January and May, first performing elaborate courtship dances that involve hopping, bobbing, bowing, bill wiping, singing and tail quivering. They lay four or five eggs in a nest shaped like a flask. Both sexes share equally in nesting duties. Three broods may be raised in each season.

CALL: Their song is a soft, tuneful whistle. A variety of other noises, such as a soft cackling, are also made.

CRIMSON FINCH

(Neochmia phaeton)

Male birds are such a striking crimson that they appear to be dipped in paint. Crimson finches are quite aggressive towards members of other family groups. They will raise their facial feathers and fan their tails. One wing is raised when fighting. Courtship and nesting of these birds is accompanied by elaborate ceremonies that include bobbing, bowing and tail quivering.

DESCRIPTION: The bill, face, throat, breast, flanks and upper tail of male birds are bright crimson, with small white spots near the wings. The crown is grey and the wings are a greyish-olive, with a crimson wash. The tail is darker and the belly and undertail is usually black, but a white-tailed form occurs in Queensland. The female is similar but olive brown above and paler below.

OTHER NAMES: Blood finch.

STATUS AND DISTRIBUTION: Crimson finches are found across northern Australia, from the Kimberley to Mackay in Queensland. They are also found in southern New Guinea.

PREFERRED HABITAT: Crimson finches inhabit wetter tropical areas, such as tall grasslands and riverine areas interspersed with screw pines (*Pandanus spiralis*) and streamside trees. It sometimes lives near settlements, because of the permanent water supply.

LIFE HISTORY: Their nests are usually constructed in screw pines but they sometimes make use of buildings. The male selects the nest and collects material but both partners help to build the feather-lined dome of grass, bark and leaves. Both help to incubate between five and eight eggs and to brood and feed the young. In WA, crimson finches breed between January and April.

CALL: They constantly chatter and call loudly, making a penetrating "tsee-tsee" sound, and have a soft rasping song.

SIGHTING RECORD

SPECIES	DATE
magpie goose	
plumed whistling-duck	
darter	
Australian pelican	
white-necked heron	
nankeen night heron	
straw-necked ibis	
jabiru	
osprey	
black kite	
white-bellied sea-eagle	
brolga	
Australian bustard	
whimbrel	
comb-crested jacana	
black-winged stilt	
black-fronted dotterel	
spinifex pigeon	
white-quilled rock-pigeon	
peaceful dove	
little corella	
rainbow lorikeet	
red-winged parrot	
budgerigar	
grey-crowned babbler	
great bowerbird	
double-barred finch	
long-tailed finch	
crimson finch	

TIME	LOCALITY	REMARKS

INDEX